Math Investigations

Ridgewood, New Jersey, Public Schools

Cathy Feldman and Barbara Peckham

BOOK 2

Educators Publishing Service, Inc.

Cambridge and Toronto

ACKNOWLEDGMENTS

Dr. Frederick J. Stokley, Superintendent of Schools in Ridgewood, New Jersey, initiated the idea of publishing Ridgewood curriculum. He hoped that Ridgewood could contribute to American education by sharing material that has proved particularly stimulating and effective in the Ridgewood schools.

Maria Sweeney, Project Manager for Ridgewood's Curriculum Publications, worked closely with the authors and publisher, as both a consultant and facilitator.

Tanya Auger, editor of the *Math Investigations* series, tested, revised, and fine-tuned the activities. She worked extensively with the Ridgewood Project Manager and the artist to pull all the pieces together.

Joan Hartmann spent long hours typing and formatting the manuscript.

Illustrations by Anne Lord
Cover design by Alicyn Sconiers

Printed in the U.S.A.
ISBN 0-8388-2353-x
August, 1997 printing

How Many?

Record.

1. Boys_____   2. Girls_____   3. Teachers_____

4. Chairs_____   5. Cubes you can hold in your hand_____

Color.

1	2	3	4	5	6	7	8	9	10
11	12	13	14	15	16	17	18	19	20
21	22	23	24	25	26	27	28	29	30
31	32	33	34	35	36	37	38	39	40
41	42	43	44	45	46	47	48	49	50
51	52	53	54	55	56	57	58	59	60
61	62	63	64	65	66	67	68	69	70
71	72	73	74	75	76	77	78	79	80
81	82	83	84	85	86	87	88	89	90
91	92	93	94	95	96	97	98	99	100

Choose 3 more objects in the room.

Write the name and number of each object.

Then color each number's box.

1. _____   _____

2. _____   _____

3. _____   _____

Race for Your School Supplies

Name _____

Birthdays

Shade in boxes.

	1	2	3	4	5	6	7	8	9	10	11	12	13	14	15
January															
February															
March															
April															
May															
June															
July															
August															
September															
October															
November															
December															

Name ______________________________

Checkers

Choose a partner. Have fun!

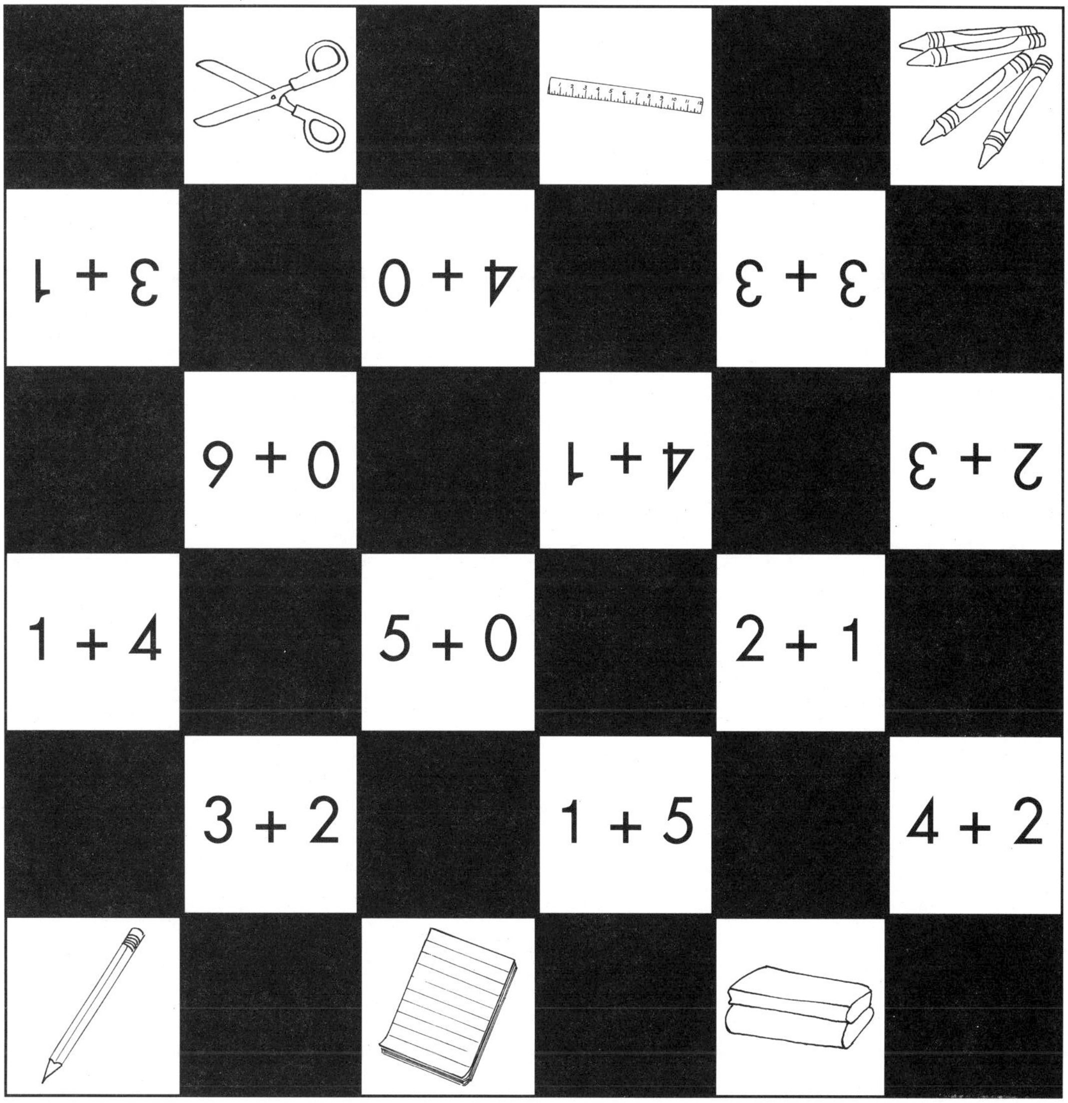
1 + 3
4 + 0
3 + 3
0 + 6
4 + 1
2 + 3
1 + 4
5 + 0
2 + 1
3 + 2
1 + 5
4 + 2

My Foot

Trace your foot.

Name _____

School Supply Patterns

Continue the patterns.

1.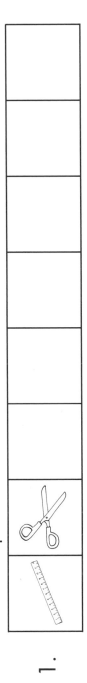

Number of repetitions: _____

2.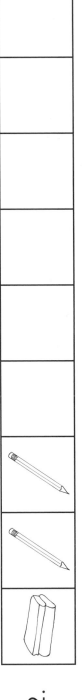

Number of repetitions: _____

Draw your own pattern of school supplies.
Cross out any squares you do not use for your pattern.

My Pattern

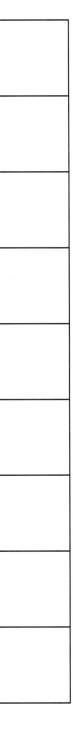

Number of repetitions: _____

Cut.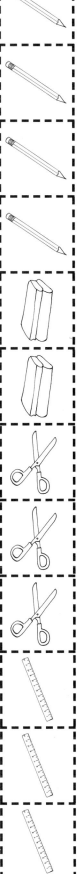

Estimate, Count, and Record Apples

Record.

Basket 1

Estimate_____

Actual_____

Basket 2

Estimate_____

Actual_____

Basket 3

Estimate_____

Actual_____

My Thinking

_____

_____

_____

_____

Combinations of 10

Color.

$\bigcirc\bigcirc\bigcirc\bigcirc\bigcirc\bigcirc\bigcirc\bigcirc\bigcirc\bigcirc$ = 10

$\bigcirc\bigcirc\bigcirc\bigcirc\bigcirc\bigcirc\bigcirc\bigcirc\bigcirc\bigcirc$ = 10

$\bigcirc\bigcirc\bigcirc\bigcirc\bigcirc\bigcirc\bigcirc\bigcirc\bigcirc\bigcirc$ = 10

$\bigcirc\bigcirc\bigcirc\bigcirc\bigcirc\bigcirc\bigcirc\bigcirc\bigcirc\bigcirc$ = 10

$\bigcirc\bigcirc\bigcirc\bigcirc\bigcirc\bigcirc\bigcirc\bigcirc\bigcirc\bigcirc$ = 10

$\bigcirc\bigcirc\bigcirc\bigcirc\bigcirc\bigcirc\bigcirc\bigcirc\bigcirc\bigcirc$ = 10

Apple Products

Shade in boxes.

14						
13						
12						
11						
10						
9						
8						
7						
6						
5						
4						
3						
2						
1						

Sorting Apples

Draw.

My observation:

Re-sorting

Draw.

My observation:

Name _____

Measure Your Apple

Record.

① I estimate that my apple is _____ inches around.

② My apple is _____ inches around.

③ The difference is _____ inches.

④ This is how I found the difference:

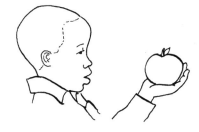

10
9
8
7
6
5
4
3
2
1

Apple Time

Color.

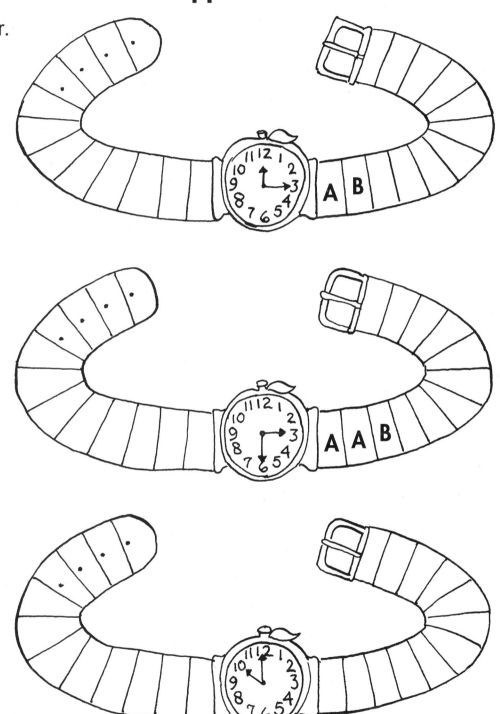

The name of my pattern is _____.

Trick-or-Treating in the Neighborhood

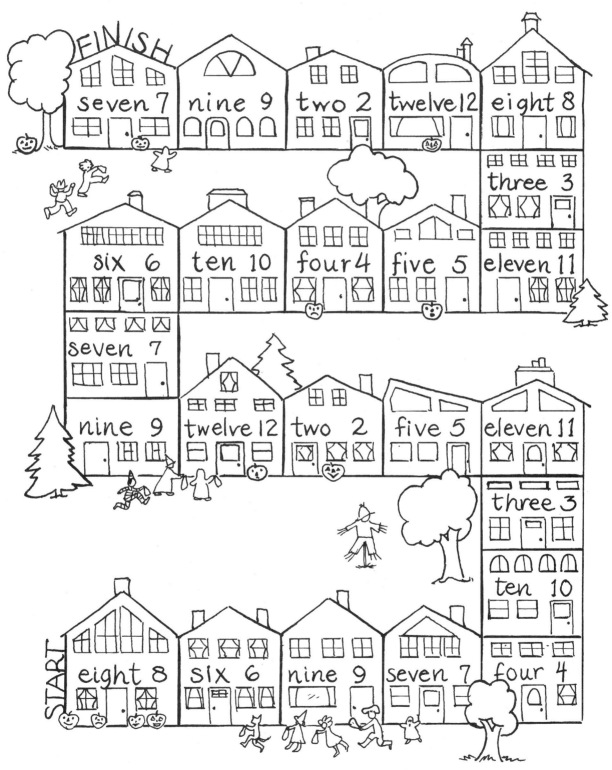

Goodie Bags

Record and add.

 +  = _____

 +  = _____

 +  = _____

 +  = _____

 + _____ = _____

Halloween Costumes

Mark an X.

	My costume makes me look silly.	My costume makes me look scary.	My costume makes me look like the real thing.
10			
9			
8			
7			
6			
5			
4			
3			
2			
1			

Making Jack-o'-lanterns

Draw.

Halloween Goodies

Record.

My name is _____.

My partner's name is _____.

I predict that _____'s bag
is heavier.

I found out that _____'s bag
is heavier.

_____'s 10 candies form a longer
line.

Name _____

Find the Pumpkin Patterns on the Calendar

Continue the pattern.

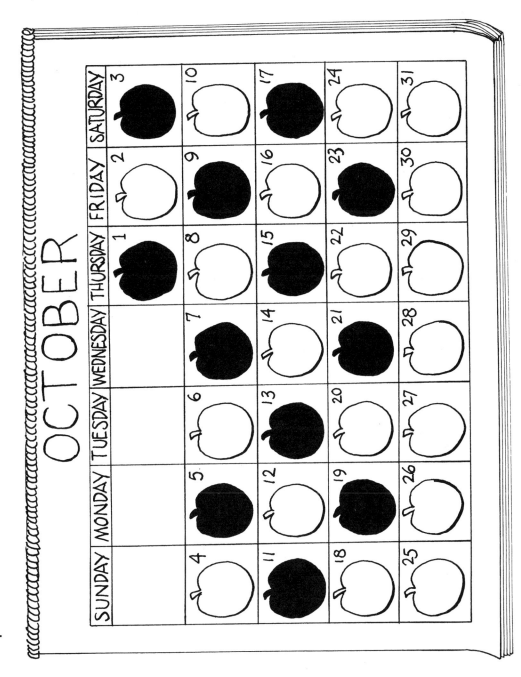

OCTOBER

SUNDAY	MONDAY	TUESDAY	WEDNESDAY	THURSDAY	FRIDAY	SATURDAY
				1	2	3
4	5	6	7	8	9	10
11	12	13	14	15	16	17
18	19	20	21	22	23	24
25	26	27	28	29	30	31

How Many Balls?

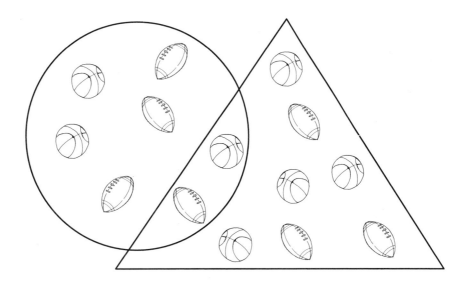

Count and record.

1. There are_____ in the circle.

2. There are_____ in the circle.

3. There are_____ in the triangle.

4. There are_____ in the triangle.

5. There are_____ and in the circle.

6. There are_____ and in the triangle.

7. There are_____ and in both the circle and the triangle.

Math Stories

Use the pictures to write 2 word problems.

1._____

_____

_____

Number sentence:_____

2._____

_____

_____

Number sentence:_____

Sports Events

Use tally marks to record.

Fun with Trading Cards

Record.

| I made a set of five trading cards. I grouped them because they all _____

 _____

 _____

 _____

 _____ | I made a second set of five trading cards. I grouped them because they all_____

 _____

 _____

 _____ |

| I made a third set of five trading cards. I grouped them because they all _____

 _____

 _____

 _____ | I made a fourth set of five trading cards. I grouped them because they all_____

 _____

 _____

 _____ |

Name _____

Let's Go Shopping

I have 75 cents to spend.

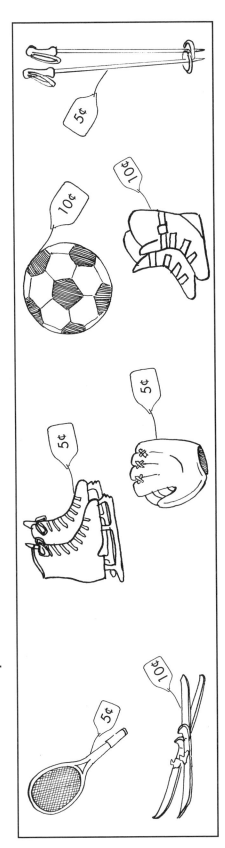

I bought:

_____ cents

_____ cents

_____ cents

_____ cents

I spent:

_____ cents

_____ + _____ = _____ cents
      already
      spent

_____ + _____ = _____ cents
      already
      spent

_____ + _____ = _____ cents
      already
      spent

I have _____ cents left over.

Sports Patterns

Cut. ✂

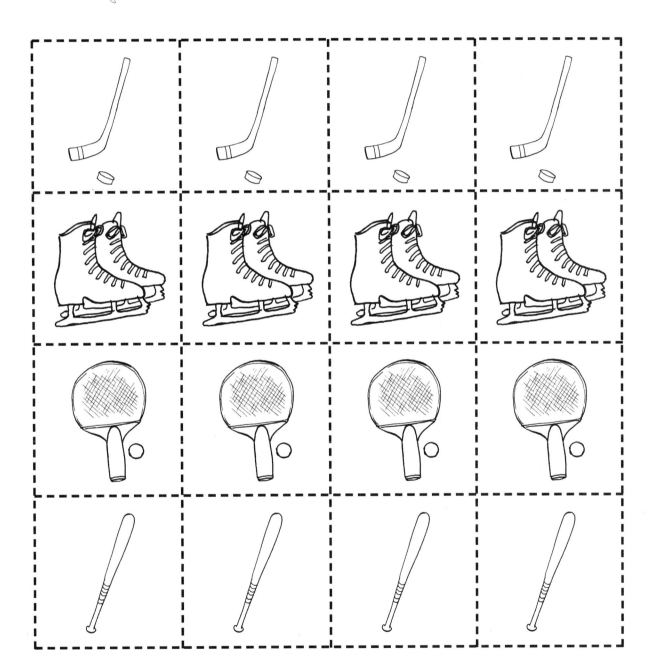

Brrr! It's Cold!

How many…?

 Buttons _____    Boots _____

 Hats _____    Mittens _____

 Coats _____    Scarves _____

If there were 2 children, how many…?

 Buttons _____    Boots _____

 Hats _____    Mittens _____

Coats _____    Scarves _____

Magic Winter Clothes

Add and record.

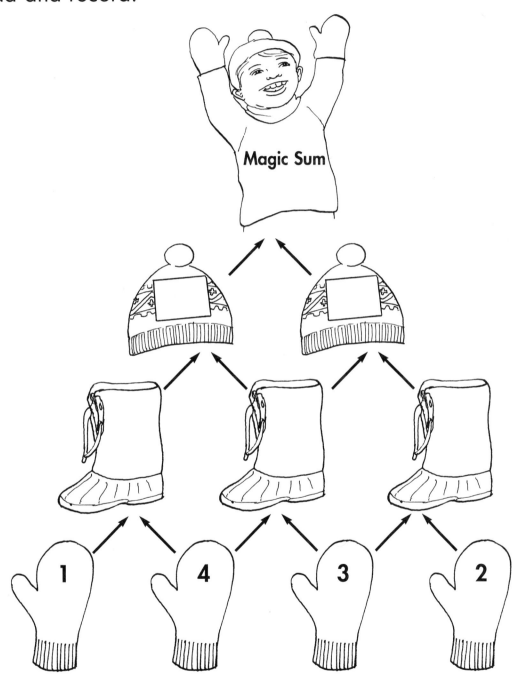

Graphing Winter Clothing

Tally.

Graph.

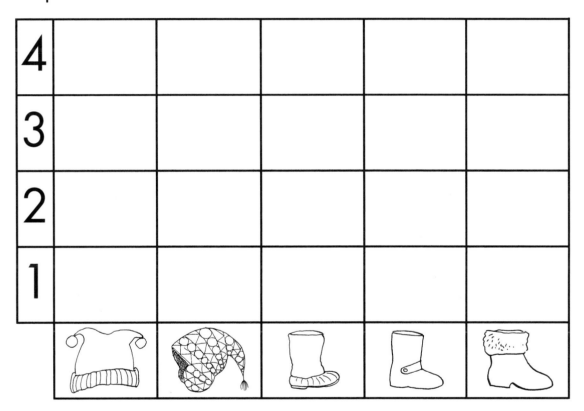

Cut. ✂

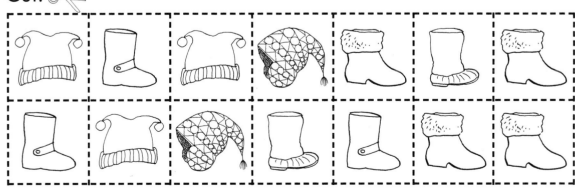

Who Lost a Mitten?

Amanda   Billy   Lisa   Jamal

Anna   DeShonda   Chris   Ming

Read each clue.
Draw a ✔ to keep your place.

The student who lost a mitten was **not**

- ☐ between two girls
- ☐ wearing glasses
- ☐ wearing a big bow
- ☐ on the bottom row

The student who lost a mitten was _____.

How Far Is It?

Use a ruler to see how far Sammy walked.

Sammy lost his hat and scarf in the snow. He walked to his hat and picked it up. Then he walked to pick up his scarf. Write and solve a number sentence to show how far Sammy walked.

_____ + _____ = _____ inches

After picking up his scarf, Sammy walked to pick up his coat. Then he walked to pick up his boots. Write and solve a number sentence to show how far Sammy walked.

_____ + _____ = _____ inches

Challenge: How far did Sammy walk in all? _____ inches

Name _____

All Wrapped Up

Show your patterns.

Name _____

Winter Counts

Skip-count and record.

14, ____, 18, ____, ____

40, ____, ____, ____, 48

____, 26, ____, 30, ____

3, ____, 9, ____, ____

42, ____, ____, 51, ____,

____, 75, ____, ____, 84

25, ____, ____, 40, ____

____, 85, ____, ____, 100

____, ____, 75, 80, ____

Calendar Fun

JANUARY

SUNDAY	MONDAY	TUESDAY	WEDNESDAY	THURSDAY	FRIDAY	SATURDAY
		1	2	3	4	5
6	7	8	9	10	11	12
13	14	15	16	17	18	19
20	21	22	23	24	25	26
27	28	29	30	31		

Find the numerals and write the number sentence.
Then solve the problem.

1. The third Wednesday minus the first Wednesday_____

2. The first Sunday plus the first Saturday_____

3. The total of all the days in the first five days_____

4. The fifth Wednesday minus the second Thursday_____

Name _____

Winter Sports Survey

Ask 15 friends: "What is your favorite winter sport?"

	Hockey	Ice Skating	Sledding	Basketball	Indoor Soccer	Skiing
15						
14						
13						
12						
11						
10						
9						
8						
7						
6						
5						
4						
3						
2						
1						

Record.

1. Which sport has the most? _____

2. Which sport has the least? _____

3. What is the difference between the two? _____

4. Make a graph of your own on the back of this page.
   Pick a topic and interview 15 friends.

Footprints in the Snow

(START)

Can you see them?
Draw a ✔ to keep your place.

☐ Five footprints to the tree

☐ Three footprints to the snowman

☐ Six footprints to the mitten

☐ Four footprints to the hat

☐ Seven footprints to the house

Time to Have Fun

What time would you...?

Go sledding _____

Build a snowman _____

Drink hot chocolate _____

Winter Pattern

Continue the pattern.

Name the pattern: _____

Cut. ✂

Name _____

Go for a Swing

Count and record.

1. How many people are in the picture? _____

2. How many people are not swinging? _____

3. How many people are swinging? _____

4. What is the total number of hands? _____

5. What is the total number of fingers? _____

Playing Around

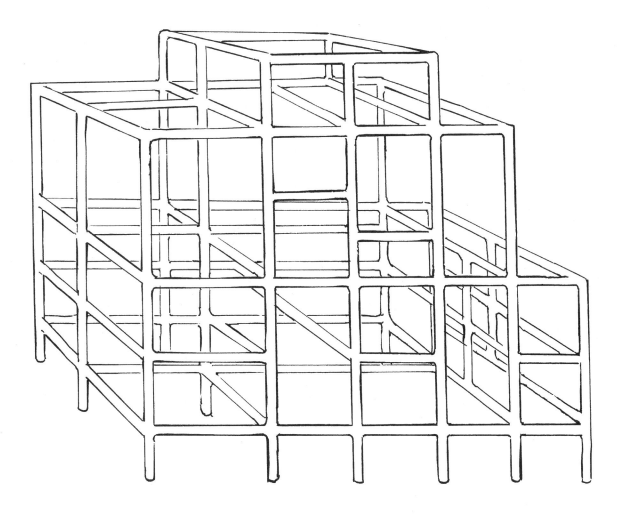

Number sentence_____ Sum_____

Cut. ✂

| 10 | 5 | 2 | 3 | 6 | 4 | 7 |

Name Graph

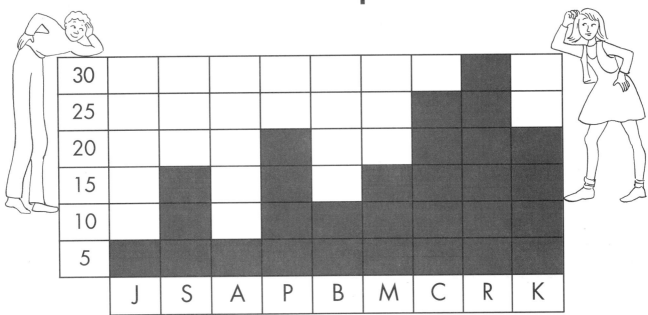

You cannot tell everything from a graph. Use the graph to answer the questions. Mark an X on the line beside the questions you **cannot** answer.

Record the number of students whose names begin with:

M _____   S + M _____

P _____   A + B _____

C _____   J + S + A _____

D _____   R + K + W _____

Name _____

Find Your Friends

Playground Fun

Glue $\frac{1}{2}$.

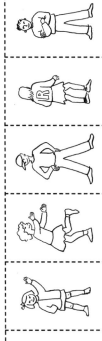

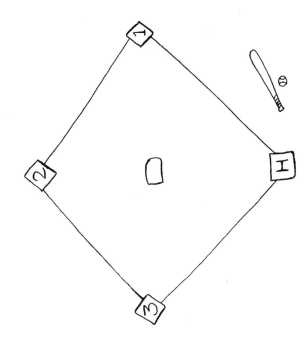

Glue $\frac{1}{2}$.

Cut. ✂

Friendship Necklace

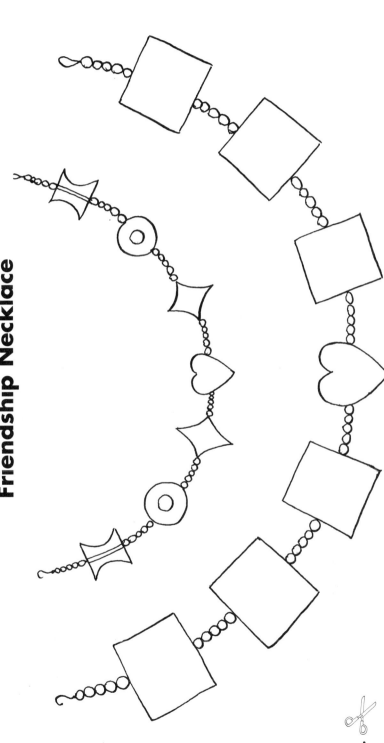

Cut. ✂

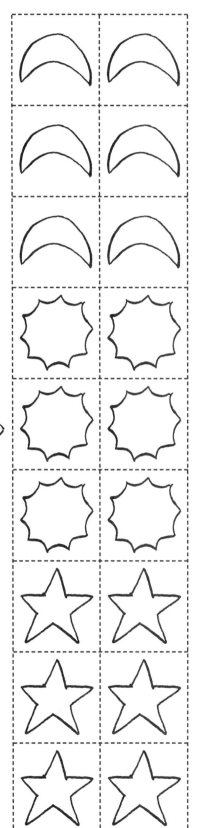

Name _____

Give Me a Hand

Trace your hand.

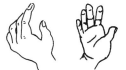

Measuring Up

Measure and record.

Neck to floor _____ _____

Knee to floor _____ _____

Shoulder to finger _____ _____

Top of head to chin _____ _____

Waist to floor _____ _____

Compute.

− ☐ Neck to floor		− ☐ Shoulder to finger
☐ Waist to floor		☐ Knee to floor
☐ _____		☐ _____

+ ☐ Head to chin		− ☐ Neck to floor
☐ Waist to floor		☐ Knee to floor
☐ _____		☐ _____

You and Me

Use tally marks to record.

Taller Than I Am	Shorter Than I Am	Same As I Am

_____ students are taller than I am.

_____ students are shorter than I am.

_____ students are the same height as I am.

Who Am I?

Read each clue.
Mark an X on the children as you eliminate them.
Then mark a ✔ to keep your place.

☐ I have short hair.

☐ I do not wear hats.

☐ Singing is not my favorite thing to do.

☐ I have a smile on my face.

☐ I wear glasses.

☐ I am a boy.

☐ Please color my picture.

Dress Me

You may spend $10.00.

Mark an X on the items you would buy to dress the child.

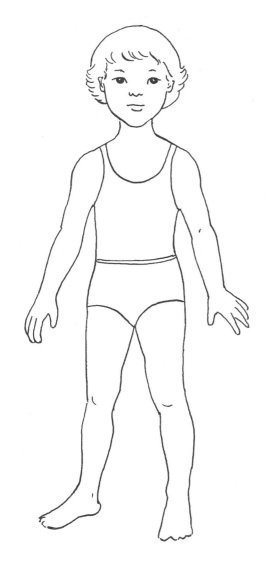

Name _____

Finish Me

Complete each picture.

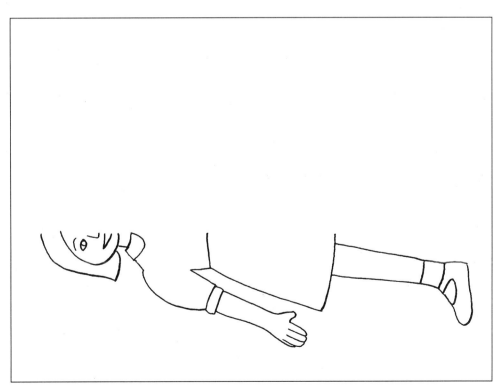

Name _____

A Garden of Odds and Evens

Write the missing numbers.
Color the odd numbers.

	62		64			67			71		73
74		76					81		84		
87	88				93		95				99

Write the missing numbers.
Color the even numbers.

33		35				40			44	45
46	47		50		53				58
59				65					71

Name _____

Stringing Along

Record.

Sums

Differences

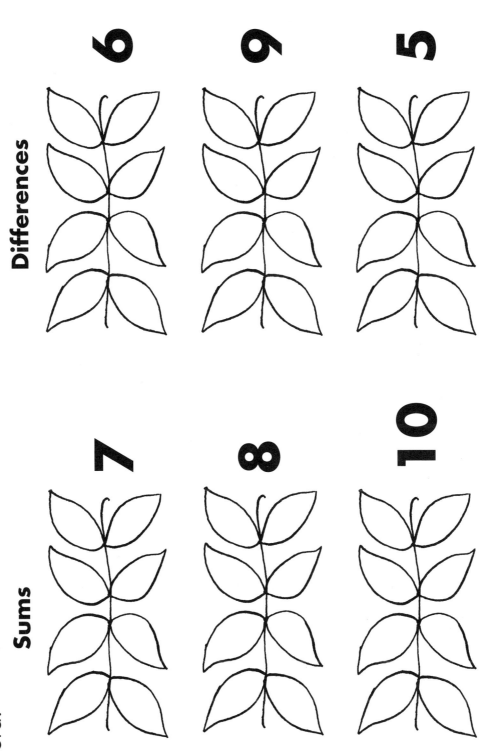

7

8

10

6

9

5

What Is Your Favorite Vegetable?

		1	2	3	4	5	6	7	8
tomatoes	🍅	▨	▨	▨	▨	▨	▨	▨	
carrots	🥕	▨	▨	▨	▨	▨	▨	▨	▨
celery	🥬	▨	▨	▨	▨				
potatoes	🥔	▨	▨	▨					

The 23 children in Mrs. Smith's class made this graph. Each child answered the question, "What is your favorite vegetable?"

Write three things you know about Mrs. Smith's class from reading the graph.

1. _____

_____

2. _____

_____

3. _____

_____

Name _____

What's Missing?

Write the missing numbers.

1.

	2	4		8	10	12	

2.

	3	6	9	12			

3.

	5	10	15		25		

4.

		20	30	40		60	

Parts of a Garden

Anna planted three vegetable gardens. She planted her favorite vegetables— 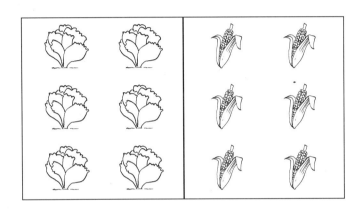 corn, carrots, and lettuce.

Circle.

1. How much of this garden did Anna plant with corn?

   $\frac{1}{2}$

   $\frac{1}{3}$

   $\frac{1}{4}$

2. How much of this garden did Anna plant with carrots?

   $\frac{1}{2}$

   $\frac{1}{3}$

   $\frac{1}{4}$

   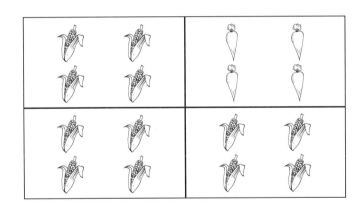

3. How much of this garden did Anna plant with lettuce?

   $\frac{1}{2}$

   $\frac{1}{3}$

   $\frac{1}{4}$

   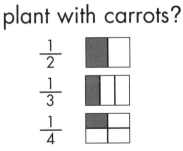
   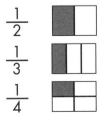

Garden Pattern

Draw.

Parade of Tens

Circle groups of ten.
Count ones.

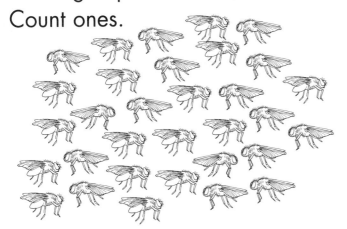

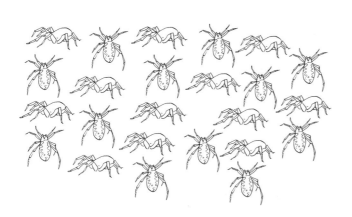

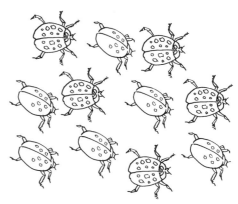

Ladybugs	Flies
Tens _____ Ones _____	Tens _____ Ones _____
Total _____	Total _____
Spiders	Butterflies
Tens _____ Ones _____	Tens _____ Ones _____
Total _____	Total _____

Name _____

Ants on the Move

You are having a picnic. Some visitors arrive—ANTS!
Draw the ants, and write a word problem about what
happens. Then write a number sentence and solve it.

Word problem: _____

_____

_____

_____

_____

Number sentence: _____

_____

Your Favorite Bug

Use tally marks to record.

Grasshopper	Ladybug	Butterfly	Lightning Bug	Other
Total				

Color.

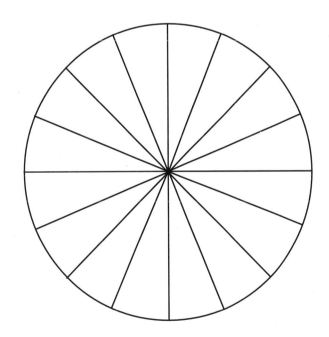

Key:

☐ Grasshopper ☐ Ladybug ☐ Butterfly

☐ Lightning Bug ☐ Other

Name _____

Circle of Critters

Cut. ✂

Crawling Around

Measure.
Write a number sentence.

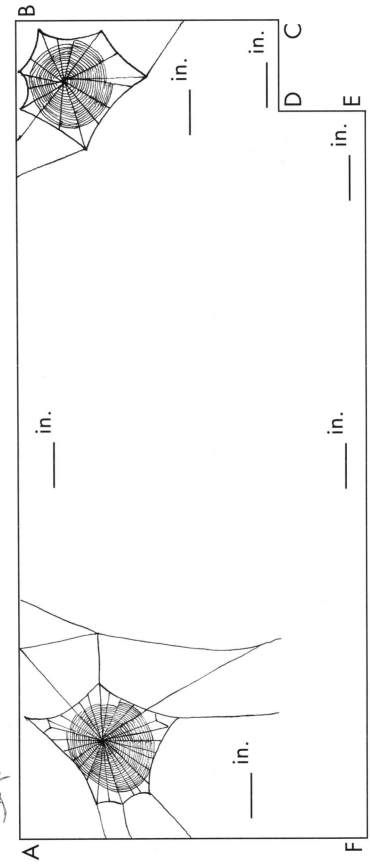

A

B

___ in.

___ in.

___ in.

D C

___ in.

E

___ in.

F

___ in.

Number sentence: _____ = _____ inches

Name _____

Caterpillar Crawl

Make the pattern RBBORBBO.... Use 16 cubes.

How many R cubes did you use? _____

How many B cubes did you use? _____

How many O cubes did you use? _____

Make the pattern YGGYGG.... Use 18 cubes.

How many Y cubes did you use? _____

How many G cubes did you use? _____

Name _____

Find the Match

Cut. ✂

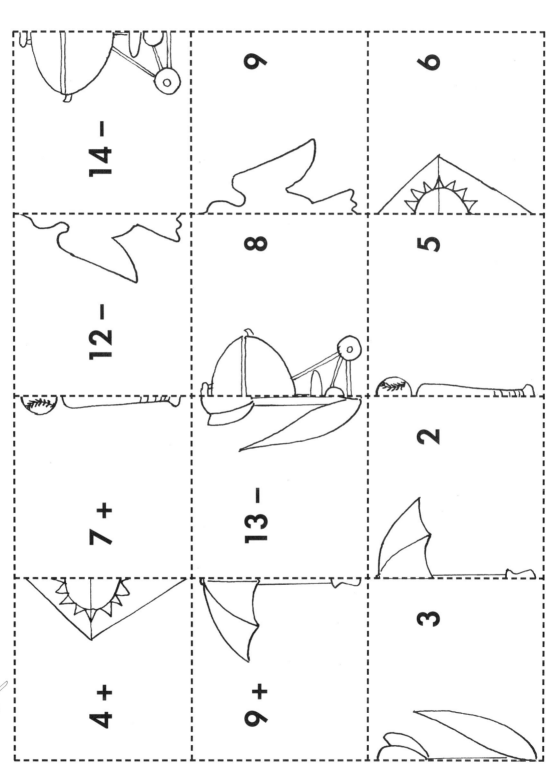

4 +	7 +	12 −	14 −
9 +	13 −	8	9
3	2	5	6

Name _____

More or Less

1. Tina has 3 basketballs. Jim has 4 more basketballs than Tina.

   Jim has _____ basketballs.

   Tina and Jim have _____ basketballs in all.

2. Marcus picked 10 flowers. Keisha picked 7 less flowers than Marcus.

   Keisha picked _____ flowers in all.

   Marcus and Keisha picked _____ flowers in all.

3. Bill played 9 games of baseball. Kate played 2 more games of baseball than Bill.

   Kate played _____ games of baseball.

   Bill and Kate played _____ baseball games in all.

4. Jose's cat had 3 kittens. John's cat had 2 more kittens than Jose's cat.

   John's cat had _____ kittens.

   Together Jose's and John's cats had _____ kittens.

Name _____

Jumping Rope

Maria										
Juan										
Joe										
Amanda										
Chris										
Samantha										

0 10 20 30 40 50 60 70 80 90 100

At the Smith School Field Day, the first grade had a great time jumping rope. Read the information and complete the graph to show how many times these six children jumped.

1. Amanda jumped 30 times.

2. Chris jumped 60 times.

3. Maria jumped 80 times.

4. Juan jumped 10 more times than Amanda.

5. Joe jumped 20 less times than Maria.

6. Samantha jumped 30 more times than Chris.

7. Who jumped the same number of times?

   _____ and _____

8. Who jumped the most?

   _____

All in a Row

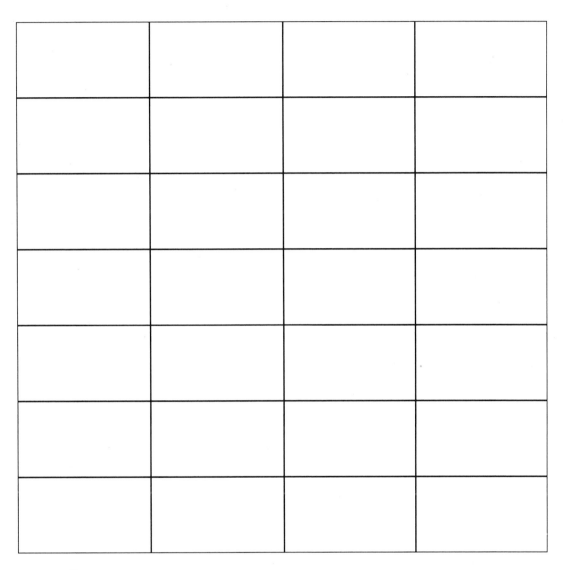

Cut. ✂

Balls of Fun

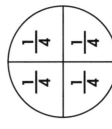
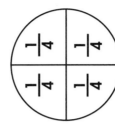
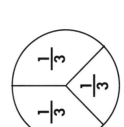

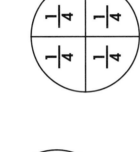

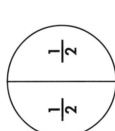

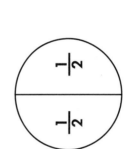

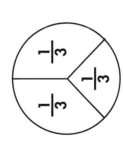

Color.

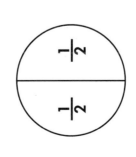

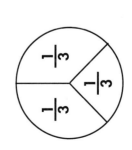

Outdoor Patterns

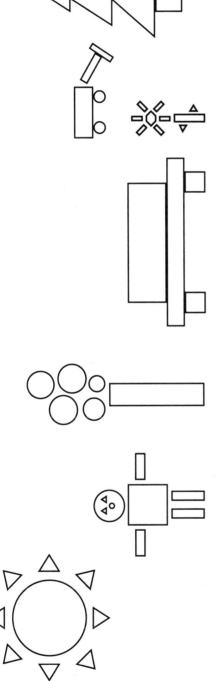

Count and record.

⬜ __ ◯ __ △ __ ▭ __ ◇ __

Add.

◯ + ▭ = __

△ + ◯ + △ = __

▭ + ◇ + ◯ = __

◯ + △ + ⬜ = __

Turn your page over, and draw your own outdoor picture using shapes.

On the Boardwalk

Use <, >, or =.

pail ☐ dog   frog ☐ dog

frog ☐ whale   pig ☐ frog

whale ☐ pony   whale ☐ frog

pony ☐ pail   dog ☐ pig

Away We Go

Use + or –.

7 □ 4 = 11

12 □ 7 = 5

9 □ 8 = 1

10 = 6 □ 4

7 □ 3 = 10

8 □ 5 = 3

12 = 8 □ 4

12 = 6 □ 6

9 □ 3 = 12

12 □ 3 = 9

10 □ 2 = 12

What Will I Need?

Make a graph.

Name _____

Which One Do I Take?

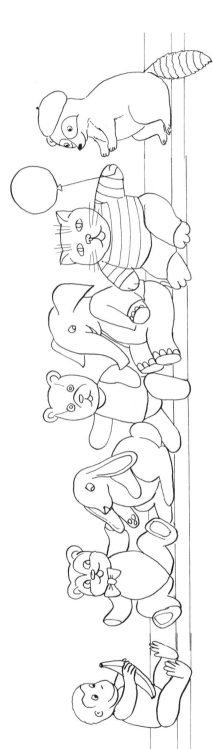

Read each clue.

Put an X on the stuffed animals as you eliminate them.

Then mark a ☑ to keep your place.

☐ I am not the middle animal.

☐ I am not holding anything.

☐ My nose is not long.

☐ I do not have long ears.

☐ I am not wearing a hat.

☐ Color me.

Money to Spend

You have 75¢ to spend.
Show three combinations
of coins that make 75¢.
Write how you came up
with the combinations.

1. 75¢

_____

_____

_____

2. 75¢

_____

_____

_____

3. 75¢

_____

_____

_____

On the Beach

Create a pattern.
Have a friend label your pattern.
Check your friend's work.